(Book 2: Books for Brand New Authors)

77 Book Marketing Ideas
for Self-Published Authors
on a Tight Budget

Michelle Emerson

Copyright © Michelle Emerson, 2020

All rights reserved

Michelle Emerson has asserted her right to be identified as the author of this Work in accordance with the Copyright, Designs and Patents Act 1988.

No part of this publication may be reproduced, stored in a retrieval system, or transmitted in any form or by any means, electronic, mechanical, photocopying, recording or otherwise, without the prior permission of the copyright owner.

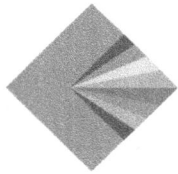

www.michelleemerson.co.uk

Brand New Books for Authors Series

1: *Finding Time to Write: How to Write More in Less Time, Embrace Your Creativity and Grab Every Opportunity to Write*

2: *77 Book Marketing Ideas for Self-Published Authors on a Tight Budget*

3: *Publish Your Book on Kindle: From Manuscript to Published on Amazon – The Simple Step-by-Step Guide*

4: *Thinking of Writing a Business Book?*

5: *30-Day Content Marketing Roadmap for Authors*

More Books by Michelle

90+ Content Ideas for Social Media, Blogs & Online Marketing

How to Write a Brilliant Business Book

100 Positive Affirmations for Writers

Dedication

This book is dedicated to all you hard-working self-published authors all over the world.

Here's to selling your books with success and confidence (without breaking the bank!).

Why Buy This Book?

Being a self-published author is amazing and frustrating all at the same time.

You spend months, even years writing your book.

You invest time and money into sourcing and hiring proofreaders and cover designers to give your book the best chance of selling.

You learn how to format your book for Kindle and print or hire someone to take care of the whole process for you.

And then bam! Before you know it, book launch day arrives.

You share your fantastic news with family, friends, colleagues, and social media followers.

And bask in the flurry of sales.

You're buzzing.

Then bam!
What the …?
The sales have stopped.

You're panicking – has all that time and money been wasted?

You can't afford to spend a fortune on ads. You can't go down the cheesy-sales-route because that's just not you.

So what can you do to sell more books?

Well, you can grab a brew and read this jam-packed, bursting-with-ideas little book for starters.

*

Designed to help you off the starting blocks, ignite new interest and intrigue in your books, and spark more ideas to help you generate sales, you'll find many a gold nugget here to make your own.

This book's

- perfect for any self-published author (regardless of genre) who's right out of book marketing ideas

- marvellous for indie authors who spend tooooo long procrastinating about lack of book sales and saturated markets

- fabulous for any aspiring self-published author who is researching book marketing ideas and wants to hit the ground running when their book is launched.

Yes, the book market's competitive, but that doesn't mean there's no room for you.

I tell all my clients to think of their book marketing journey as a marathon rather than a sprint. It's a trial and error journey for all of us.

So take your time and test out different ideas. Even the ones you think aren't really for you. I know we're all different and as an introvert myself, I know that shouting about my book is something I prefer to do from a keyboard, rather than in front of a crowd. You may be the same. But see which ideas work for you. Put your own stamp on them.

Don't forget to keep a record of what works, too! Because then you can repeat the successful promo ideas in a few months' time.

Above all else, be consistent with your marketing. And keep writing and publishing more books too!

Unless you're a keyword expert, or you have a limitless advertising budget (and you know how to convert ads into book sales) your royalties will dry up.

And you didn't put all that effort into writing and publishing your book just to let it gather dust on the Amazon shelves.

To get the best from this book...

Read the entire book once. Yes, it will spark heaps of ideas during the first read. But you'll get heaps more if you read and digest the contents before you start implementing.

Once you're familiar with these 77 simple promo ideas, **play lucky dip with the book.** Decide to do one task every day from the book and tick it off as you go. If you can't decide which idea to try, flick through the pages (or e-pages) randomly. Stop wherever the finger of fate leads you.

Buy a new notebook and dedicate it to your book marketing ideas. Even better (ahem!) (check out *My Book Promotion Ideas* notebook from Amazon).

My Book Promotion Ideas: The Blank Notebook for Indie Authors/Self-Published Authors to Organise Their Book Marketing Strategies (Planners for Indie Authors)

This way your ideas will be in one place (no scrappy notes here, there and everywhere) and you have a notebook to take wherever you go (because inspiration strikes when you least expect it!).

Grab a pen or pencil once you're ready for your second read-through because as well as the 77 book marketing ideas for you to implement, I've also added questions, prompts and extra resources for you to check out.

Create a book marketing plan. Use your favourite ideas to form the basis of a book marketing plan that you can tweak and build on time and time again.

Take action. Don't let this be another empty promises book. Don't pop it on your bookshelf and become another one of those boring indie authors who moans all the time about their book not selling.

You ready to start?

Let's go!

Book Marketing Idea #1

ADD A LINK TO YOUR BOOK IN YOUR EMAIL SIGNATURE.

How many emails do you send out while wearing your 'author' hat? Use this opportunity to share a link to your book.

Want to disguise the lengthy Amazon link address? Use Bitly or another link shortening tool.

And instead of sharing a boring link, make it more compelling, eg: *'Did you check out the free sample of my book yet on Amazon?'* and hide the hyperlink behind the words.

Book Marketing Idea #2

SET UP AN AUTHOR PAGE ON SOCIAL MEDIA.

Start with whichever platform you know best and/or where you know your ideal readers hang out.

My first choice is Facebook because my target audience is there and this is where I feel most confident posting and engaging.

Once you're set up, monitor it, and if it's working, fantastic. If not, try another social media platform..

And if your book's targeted at business people, try LinkedIn – here's my link if you'd like to connect: www.linkedin.com/in/selfpublishingservicesuk

Book Marketing Idea #3

START A NEWSLETTER.

If you don't send out a regular newsletter yet then what better excuse to start?

Staying in regular touch with your newsletter subscribers means you're able to share news of upcoming books, your reviews, future ideas and keep building relationships.

I use Mailchimp (the free version) as my email marketing software and it's easy to navigate (even if you're not techy). But there are many other options, so see which works best for your needs.

Book Marketing Idea #4

BUILD AN ONLINE COMMUNITY.

An online community of people who read your books is invaluable. If you don't fancy the idea of setting up a newsletter and writing to them regularly, this is a good (and simpler) free alternative.

All you have to do is, for example, set up a Facebook Group and add a link to your book(s) saying something like:

'Want to keep in touch? Then join my free and fabulous Facebook group where you can find out what I'm up to, get first dibs on my next book, and help me decide on my next book cover. Here's the link.'

Book Marketing Idea #5

ADD A FREE CHALLENGE TO YOUR BOOK.

If you've written a non-fiction book that teaches people a new skill then think what the next simple step would be for them once they've read your book.

Could you turn this into a free 5-day challenge?

Fab! This means they'll give you their email address, they'll continue to follow you even after they've finished reading and it could encourage them to join your online community too.

Book Marketing Idea #6

BE A GUEST SPEAKER.

Whether it's a guest speaker at a local networking event, community centre/parish hall or writer's group, you'll be welcomed with open arms.

Local groups are always looking to introduce new and interesting people to their groups.

So do some research and start off with any local opportunities. When you're feeling braver search a bit wider – county-wide, regional and national.

Who knows where your guest slot might lead.

Book Marketing Idea #7

SELL YOUR BOOK FACE-TO-FACE.

Buy a small stash of your books at the reduced author rate and sell signed copies face-to-face.

Take them to networking events or workshops or writer's groups if you attend them.

People are inquisitive by nature so if you have two or three copies of your book, you can let them see, touch, smell (or is that just me?) and flick through it before they buy.

Book Marketing Idea #8

HAVE A 'VIRTUAL' BOOK PARTY ON SOCIAL MEDIA.

Once you've got your author page set up on social media, have a virtual book party.

Invite anyone and everyone you know – including your book buyers, your editor, cover designer and/or the people who have joined your private communities – and talk about your book.

Show them the cover, talk about how long the book took to write/create and what the type of results they can expect once they've read it (if it's non-fiction). If it's a novel/children's book, talk about the characters, the setting and why you were inspired to write the story. And always talk about the sequel or the next one in the series if you've got one planned.

Book Marketing Idea #9

INTERACT WITH BOOK BLOGGERS.

Put a simple 'where to find book bloggers UK' search into Google. See who they are and what genre they specialise in.

Many have email lists you can subscribe to and that's a non-committal way to see if you like their writing/opinions and reviews, and/or whether they are a good fit to get in touch with.

Book Marketing Idea #10

APPROACH KEY INFLUENCERS IN YOUR GENRE.

Discover who the key influencers are in your niche/genre. You can do this simply by adding a keyword to Google. For example, if you've written about past-life regression, put that term/keyword phrase into Google and see who comes up.

Spend time researching the influencer's social media pages, comment on their posts and sign up to their lists to find out more about them.

Only when there's an opportunity to send them a free copy of your book in exchange for a review, do so. Don't direct message them with a hard sell otherwise you'll be ignored and potentially blocked.

Book Marketing Idea #11

SHARE EXCERPTS FROM YOUR BOOK ON SOCIAL MEDIA.

This is a great tactic to pique the interest of potential readers. Pick a nice, comfy armchair, organise your book reading in advance (and invite people along to virtually join you) and tell them part of the story.

Remember to make the buying process easy too. Add a *buy here* link to the comments underneath your Facebook live or your YouTube video.

Book Marketing Idea #12

CREATE MEMES FROM YOUR BOOK AND SHARE ON SOCIAL MEDIA.

Memes are easy to create and powerful when shared.

Use a free and simple tool like Canva (www.canva.com) to create yours.

Spend half an hour deciding on your memes and another creating them and that's a great hour's investment of your time which could get your book in front of more potential buyers.

Book Marketing Idea #13

JOIN A WRITING GROUP.

There's nothing quite so isolating as writing. But it doesn't have to be a solitary experience.

Join a local writing group or a virtual one if that's more your scene.

This gives you a chance to speak with like-minded people and potentially an opportunity to share your book.

In case you missed the chance before, you'd be very welcome to join my free virtual Facebook Group, The Writer's Sanctuary. We share links to our books too.

Book Marketing Idea #14

BUILD A ONE-PAGE WEBSITE.

This isn't quite as tricky or costly as you think.

Keep it simple by adding just a few sections:

- Welcome
- About the Author
- Your Books
- Connect with the Author

To get started, simply Google: 'How to set up a one-page website for free'. I'd highly recommend starting with WordPress.

Book Marketing Idea #15

JOIN 'FREE BOOK PROMO' SOCIAL MEDIA GROUPS.

There are so many different groups you could join, particularly on Facebook, that I'm not going to list them here.

Obviously, some will not be a good fit for you, so spend a little time finding free promo groups which feel right and start sharing your book(s) as often as you like.

Book Marketing Idea #16

START BLOGGING.

Content marketing, particularly blogging is an excellent, free and easy way to promote your book.

Not only will you be able to show off your writing and storytelling skills through your blog but you'll also build up relationships (and the know, like and trust factor) with potential readers who may become loyal followers.

Don't worry if you don't have a website. You can publish them on LinkedIn and on Medium. Both are free and easy to set up.

Book Marketing Idea #17

WRITE GUEST BLOGS.

There are heaps of benefits to guest blogging (check out this article on my website: michelleemerson.co.uk/big-beautiful-benefits-guest-blogging/

Consistent, high quality guest blogs can do wonders for the longevity of your author reputation and potentially your book sales.

Add your book's link in your bio but don't make your guest blog overly salesy. Rather, make it fitting for your host and in a way that links naturally to your book.

I'm always happy to share guest blogs on my website so get in touch if you'd like to be considered.

Book Marketing Idea #18

BUILD RELATIONSHIPS ONLINE AND OFFLINE.

Book lovers are always on the lookout for a new book recommendation. So make sure your friends and family know about your books, as well as any colleagues. Word of mouth recommendations are the best!

If you network in 'real life' at business events, make sure you have 'Author' and/or your book title on your business card.

When you're online, add 'Author' to your bio on social media platforms. It's always a great conversation starter and who knows where this will lead.

Book Marketing Idea #19

SET UP A YOUTUBE CHANNEL.

It's free, it's easy and it's quick to set up. And it's also great way to sell your books.

Need I say more?

Check out Dave Chesson's article about using YouTube as a book marketing tool here:

https://kindlepreneur.com/youtube-sell-books/

Book Marketing Idea #20

APPROACH LOCAL SHOPS, CAFES OR COMMUNITY ORGANISATIONS.

Whether you've written a local interest book or not, it's a good idea to approach any shops, cafes or community organisations in your locality to see if they would stock your books on a sale or return basis.

Small, local, independent places that you frequent regularly are a particularly good avenue to tap into.

I have an author who actually left a stash of his memoirs in the local butcher's. He didn't think they would sell, but two hours after leaving them, he received a call from the butcher to ask for more. He'd sold 7 copies!

Book Marketing Idea #21

REVISIT YOUR KEYWORDS.

If your book sales have dried up then log into your KDP dashboard (or whichever platform you've used to publish your book) and take a look at the keywords you chose originally.

Are there any blatantly obvious WRONG keywords in there? Have they been spelt incorrectly (easily done, by the way)?

Do they feel outdated now your book's been published for a while?

Do some research into keywords and make the appropriate changes.

Book Marketing Idea #22

RELOCATE YOUR CATEGORIES.

While you're making changes to your keywords, you can also revisit your categories.

If your book's in a 'General' or 'Thriller' or 'Contemporary Romance' category then it's got a heck of a lot of competition to contend with.

Try instead to find something unique about your book and add it to a less competitive category. Eg: if your novel features a Native American, add it to the Native American fiction category.

Did you know that you can add your book in up to 10 categories on Amazon KDP? Contact them direct to find out the process.

Book Marketing Idea #23

REHASH YOUR DESCRIPTION/BLURB.

A poorly written blurb/Amazon description is not going to sell your book.

If you struggle with this, read through the descriptions and blurbs of other books in your genre to see the kind of styles that grab your attention and pull you in.

I love Bryan Cohen's book: *How to Write a Sizzling Synopsis.*

Here's a link to it on Amazon if you'd like to check it out: https://amzn.to/382CvxI

Book Marketing Idea #24

RE-DESIGN YOUR BOOK COVER.

Again, a new and updated book cover can do wonders for your book sales. I know.

I changed the cover of my book <u>*90+ Content Ideas for Social Media, Blogs & Online Marketing.*</u> And after a few months' dry spell, it started selling again.

Look at the book covers in your genre/niche.

Does your cover pale in comparison?

Could you give it a simple but effective makeover in Canva.com?

Book Marketing Idea #25

WRITE ANOTHER BOOK! CREATE A SERIES.

Those who succeed with good sales are often authors who write a series of books.

This doesn't just have to be fiction.

It can work for non-fiction books too. You can write a whole series of short and sweet books in your niche (5k words is enough for an ebook – this one is just under 8k).

And always remember to list all your book titles (plus the 'Coming Soon' ones) in the front of your book to make potential buyers aware of them (and make good use of the Amazon 'Look Inside' feature).

Book Marketing Idea #26

LOCAL RADIO.

One for the extroverts!

Is there a local radio or community station nearby?

They are often looking to champion authors and the stories behind their books, particularly if you're a local lad/lass.

Listen to the radio station (if you don't already) and/or look up their schedules if possible. You might just spot an opportunity.

Get in touch and see where it leads.

Book Marketing Idea #27

TRY YOUR LOCAL NEWSPAPER.

If you're more of an introvert, you can still promote your book in the local media.

Get a copy of your local newspaper or community paper or parish news and see if an article about you and your book would prove in line with their content and articles.

If you are lucky enough to be featured, make sure the reader knows where and how to buy a copy of your book too.

Book Marketing Idea #28

CREATE VIDEOS.

Creating videos to show your book to the world via social media or your website doesn't have to cost anything but time and patience.

I use the free version of Screencast-O-Matic which allows you to record a video for up to 15 minutes.

There is a Screencast-O-Matic logo on all my videos but I don't see that as a problem.

The paid option is fairly inexpensive too, check out the website for up-to-date rates.

Book Marketing Idea #29

REGULARLY ASK FOR REVIEWS.

As well as having a page in all of your books (ebooks and paperbacks) asking for a review, you should request them regularly via your social media platforms.

Shy bairns get nowt as they say in my neck of the woods. (You don't ask, you don't get.)

Or if anyone contacts you personally to tell you how much they enjoyed your book, ask them to leave a review on Amazon.

Us authors rely on reviews, so don't be afraid to ask for them regularly on social media too. And invest in the karma bank too by leaving reviews of books you've read and loved.

Book Marketing Idea #30

SIGN UP FOR AMAZON AUTHOR CENTRAL.

Amazon Author Central is a great marketing tool. It's a place for any passing potential reader to see all your books, read your bio, see your mugshot and watch your videos.

Set up a page in each country you sell your book in too. If you're UK-based, I'd highly recommend setting up a US (.com) page. You can add your RSS feed (blog link) to your profile and all your latest blogs are featured. This results in many US sales for me (more than the UK actually) and lots of US visitors to my website.

Start here:
https://authorcentral.amazon.com/gp/help

Book Marketing Idea #31

LINK YOUR BOOK TO HOT / TRENDING TOPICS.

If there's an opportunity to link your book to a trending topic on social media, grab it.

Get into the habit of checking every day to see what's trending on any and every social media platform you have a presence on.

Link your book to the trending topic or hashtag and then sit back and see what happens.

Book Marketing Idea #32

CREATE YOUR BOOKS IN EVERY FORMAT.

If you only publish your book in one format (eg paperback) you'll miss out on potential extra royalties.

Creating a kindle version of your printed book is great for people (like me) who aren't patient enough to wait for Royal Mail. It's also great for your royalties too because you get way more return on ebooks than paperbacks - there are no printing costs).

Could you think about creating an audio version too?

Book Marketing Idea #33

NETWORK.

Network online by joining social media groups and book/indie author/self-publishing forums.

Sign up to online groups that are geared towards your book's niche, too. For example, if you've written a business guide for holistic therapists, make sure you're in plenty of holistic therapist groups.

Offline networking is valuable for authors too. See what's available in your locality and/or (as I mentioned in #13) consider joining a writing group.

Book Marketing Idea #34

ENTER YOUR BOOK INTO A COMPETITION.

There are all kinds of competitions around and entering your book into them is easy. Often, there's no fee to pay either. If there is, then choose your competitions wisely.

Check out writing magazines as they are always running competitions.

You never know what could happen!

Good luck!

Book Marketing Idea #35

SIGN UP TO GOODREADS.

You can join Goodreads, as an author, for free, regardless of where you are in the world.

It's a hugely popular virtual space to engage with readers and promote your books.

Here's the link to find out more:

https://www.goodreads.com/author/program

Book Marketing Idea #36

LEARN FROM THE BEST.

Who are your favourite best-selling authors?

Who do you love who writes in your genre or for your niche?

Check out their platforms, websites and books.

Listen to their podcasts.

Sign up to their newsletters.

Discover how they market their books, what tactics they use to pull in their readers and see if you could implement the same in your promo strategy.

Book Marketing Idea #37

DONATE YOUR BOOK TO SHOPS.

As well as donating a copy of your book to your local charity shop, see if any supermarkets or other shops have a designated charity book exchange.

If you do this, pop a little note into your book or a bookmark explaining that you're a local author and you'd love for anyone who's read this book to donate it back to another local charity shop to see if the cycle can continue.

This isn't just a lovely case of paying it forward, it's also an opportunity to build your author reputation.

Book Marketing Idea #38

SET UP GOOGLE ALERTS RELATED YOUR BOOK'S TOPIC.

Does that sound too techy? Don't be put off, it isn't complicated. A Google alert is just like any customised search you'd carry out on Google (or any other search engine, in fact).

The results are sent to you automatically via email and are a super tool to help you monitor any online activity (news, videos, blogs etc) based upon whatever search term is important to you and/or relevant to your book which you can then use as social media content and link to your book at the same time.

Get started here: https://google.com/alerts

Book Marketing Idea #39

SOCIAL PROOF - MAKE MEMES OF YOUR REVIEWS/TESTIMONIALS.

I've mentioned Canva a few times now but it's so easy and it's free.

Creating simple memes of your reviews and/or testimonials (if you've written a specialist non-fiction book) or even excerpts from your books are great marketing fodder to keep in your archives and rotate time and time again.

Book Marketing Idea #40

HOLD A COMPETITION/GIVEAWAY.

Doing this online means you'll not just:

1. boost audience engagement on your posts
2. capture more email addresses
3. potentially get more likes/followers on your social media platforms

but it could also help you sell more books in the short and long term.

Book Marketing Idea #41

SHARE PHOTOS OF PEOPLE READING YOUR BOOK.

Obviously, you'll need to add a request to your book's interior and ask people to do this.

Give it a try, it can be great fun. I've seen it in action.

Even better, run a competition for people to vote for their favourite picture and give them a free book as the prize.

Book Marketing Idea #42

Research local opportunities.

Have you written a specialist book that would appeal to the locals?

For example, where I live, a company who specialise in investigating the paranormal have recently published a book. I don't know how much promo they've done but I do see it around everywhere – cafes, the library and even in my hairdresser's (I haven't checked the butcher's out yet, though).

If a copy of their book is placed in each of the establishments they've mentioned, then they'll probably be happy to sell the books for them too.

Definitely worth considering for your book.

Book Marketing Idea #43

PROMOTE YOUR BOOK ON THE FREE PROMOTION SITES.

Yes, this will take a bit of researching and organising but it's worth a shot.

Some of these free book promo sites (that's the term you should Google) also have a free submission tool so you don't have to keep entering the same information hundreds of times.

Keep a record of any which work for you.

Book Marketing Idea #44

APPROACH YOUR LOCAL BOOKSTORE.

Like I've mentioned previously, offering your books on a sale or return basis to bookstores you know and love could prove fruitful for you.

Try your nearest 'Waterstone's too. Very often they have a designated section for local authors. I once edited a charity children's book for a school in Durham (*The Adventures of William the Bear* – a very smart bear who travelled the world with the Royal Navy and got up to all sorts of adventures) and they were kind enough to let us have a book launch there and sell copies of the book too.

Book Marketing Idea #45

ESTABLISH AND BUILD A SOLID AUTHOR BRAND.

Look on your book promo as a business. You wouldn't expect new clients to find you if you weren't actively promoting your business, would you? Same goes for your book.

Make sure everything about your author brand is professional and recognisable, that your social media posts and content are tasteful, well-written and a good mix of words and images.

Even if you are a hobbyist self-publisher who writes from a cubbyhole at the back of your kitchen, you can still project a top quality, professional image.

Book Marketing Idea #46

MAKE IT EASY FOR YOUR POTENTIAL BUYERS TO BUY.

I see many authors promoting their books with persuasive social media posts and blogs etc but then they don't make it easy for their readers to buy.

You need to have a big BUY NOW! button that stands out a mile. Make it flash or sing or dance or sparkle!

Don't say things like, 'You can buy this in Kindle format from Amazon' because unless someone is really desperate to bag a copy of your book, they won't bother to cut and paste the details into the Amazon store. So make it easy and they'll buy.

Book Marketing Idea #47

KNOW YOUR AUDIENCE INSIDE OUT.

You'll already know your audience inside out if you did your research properly before you wrote the book.

So go and hang out where they are.

If your book's about handling the terrible twos, go and join the Facebook groups where these stressed out yummy mummies like to let off steam.

Many social media groups have a free promo day – so write the day in your diary.

Book Marketing Idea #48

HAVE A VIRTUAL BOOK LAUNCH.

You know the day your book's launching, right? So as well as having a virtual book party (see #8) you could also build up a buzz and have an online book launch for your social media followers.

Tell them it's going to be at 8pm on Wednesday 22nd January and they can watch from the comfort of their own sofa.

Make sure you embed the Facebook Live on your website, newsletter or YouTube channel or into a blog and/or on other social media to maximise its sales potential.

Book Marketing Idea #49

ADD 'AUTHOR OF ...' TO ALL YOUR SOCIAL MEDIA BIOS.

Adding 'Author' to your LinkedIn bio, for example, is searchable.

So if people are specifically looking for an author in the UK who's written a historical novel set in the 19th century and you're her (or him) and this kind of info is in your bio, guess what? They're going to connect with you and you can start building up the know, like and trust factor – and then they'll start buying your books.

Book Marketing Idea #50

DO A 'BOOK BOX OPENING' VIDEO.

Personally, these make me cringe when they're overdone. But hey ho, this isn't about me so I'm just putting this idea out there for you.

If you've never seen one before, you'll find plenty on YouTube. And if it looks fun and like your cup of tea, then go do it.

All jesting aside, they are fab for creating a buzz, getting potential buyers interested in your book, and letting people see the real person behind the 'author' tag.

Book Marketing Idea #51

APPROACH BOOK BLOGGERS/REVIEWERS.

Following on from #19, if you find book bloggers you like, then reach out to them.

They're very social people and often host interviews, competitions and giveaways on their blog sites. Finding a book blogger you click with could prove really beneficial to your book business.

Many book reviewers charge fees to read your book and offer guarantees of book sales or your money back. So go and investigate if you think this is a good option to try.

Book Marketing Idea #52

SELL YOUR BOOK AT FAIRS, FETES AND FESTIVALS.

If you've written a book in the Mind/Body/Spirit genre, see if you can hire a table at a Mind/Body/Spirit fair. A captive audience with a strong interest in your subject awaits.

Similarly, sell your children's books at school fetes or Christmas markets.

And if you're a Pilates teacher with a Pilates book for beginners, then make sure you're at the local authority's latest Wellbeing Festival or annual show armed with your books.

Book Marketing Idea #53

BE AN INTERVIEWEE ON A PODCAST.

The world has gone podcast crazy and it's a helpful way to get in front of an audience who are interested in your specialist subject/your story or your background.

For example, if you're a single dad bringing up two kids under the age of 5 and you've written a book about it, you could be a fascinating prospect for a professional podcaster who talks about parenting.

All it takes is a little research to find the right podcaster for you.

Book Marketing Idea #54

START YOUR OWN PODCASTS.

It's not as tricky as you might think and it really could be the breakthrough you need when it comes to selling your books.

Here's a nifty guide that walks you through every step of the set-up process from Podcast Insights:

https://www.podcastinsights.com/start-a-podcast/

Book Marketing Idea #55

USE HASHTAGS ON SOCIAL MEDIA.

If you've written a book about self-publishing you'll find all kinds of related hashtags floating around on social media.

#selfpublishing   #indieauthor

These hashtags are simply shortcuts so that people looking for a particular subject (which you cover in your book) can find information quickly on social media.

Make a list of hashtags that are relevant to your book and test them out on your favourite social media platforms.

Book Marketing Idea #56

COMMENT ON SOCIAL MEDIA POSTS TO ESTABLISH & BUILD YOUR AUTHOR REPUTATION/EXPERTISE.

Posting and engaging on social media isn't just about coming up with content. You can get so many more eyes on your brand, your books, and your author platforms if you join in conversations.

Spend 10-15 minutes a day liking, commenting and engaging on posts and see how much of a difference it can make to your visibility. This, in turn, can provide a foundation for future book sales.

Book Marketing Idea #57

FIND & NURTURE YOUR TRIBE.

If you've written a book about overcoming adversity, set up a Facebook group and build a community of like-minded people.

Not only will these people be potential book buyers, but you'll also be creating a private place to share, engage and support people through sticky spots.

This could lead to all other kinds of opportunities too – story anthologies of all the group members and more juicy stuff like that.

Book Marketing Idea #58

USE QUORA.

Spark a conversation about a topic related to your book by using www.quora.com. Use keywords or key phrases in your question and write an article about it.

For example, ask the question: 'What are the benefits of journaling?' and you'll see articles with links to journal templates in the sign-off.

This could work for you and your book, too.

Book Marketing Idea #59

START AN 'ASK ME ANYTHING ABOUT WRITING/PUBLISHING/YOUR SPECIALIST SUBJECT' LIVE SESSION ON SOCIAL MEDIA.

Even if doing Facebook Lives are your worst nightmare, this is still a good habit to get into.

Not only will Lives boost engagement and potentially book sales, but they also allow people to see the real you. Your quirks, your sense of humour, your knowledge, your personality.

It's much easier to resonate with (and buy from) a real person than just text-based posts. And when people connect with you, they buy.

Book Marketing Idea #60

JOIN BOOKBUB.

Establishing a presence as an author on BookBub is a good marketing tactic.

It's an effective way to drive traffic to your books, your website and/or your Amazon Author Central page (and super for SEO too).

Visit BookBub.com or click this link to claim your author profile: https://partners.bookbub.com/author_profile_claims/new

Book Marketing Idea #61

DO A BOOK SIGNING
- VISIT YOUR LOCAL BOOKSHOP.

A book signing is another up close and personal opportunity for your readers to connect with you.

Not only that, but it's a fab chance to get to know them (what does your reader demographic look like – how can you build on that in the future?), ask questions about their interest in your book/subject and encourage more word of mouth sales (you've created a memory with them and they'll be dying to share it with their nearest and dearest).

Book Marketing Idea #62

SIGN UP TO KDP SELECT.

Amazon have created this opt-in programme for authors to offer their books for free for a limited time (90 days) where you agree to exclusivity with them.

I know you're thinking, how can this be marketing when I won't get paid? Look into it.

Particularly if you've created a series of books and/or you have another about to launch. Or if you have created a business book that you just want to use as a free lead magnet (add the links to your book). Take a look and see if it's a good option for you.

Book Marketing Idea #63

ADD YOUR BOOK(S) TO YOUR FACEBOOK AUTHOR PAGE.

There's a section on your business/author Facebook page called 'shop'.

Make sure you add your books to it.

Use DIY book covers to create a super professional looking 3D image, set up a PayPal link if you want to send them to your website for a PDF download or direct them to your book's Amazon sales page.

Book Marketing Idea #64

ADD YOUR BOOK DETAILS TO THE APPROPRIATE SECTION ON LINKEDIN.

If you have a presence on LinkedIn, there's a section in your profile to add 'Publications'.

What better place to add your books?

Click on your profile > scroll down to Accomplishments and then add your book's title, blurb and your Amazon link. Simple.

Book Marketing Idea #65

DONATE A COPY TO YOUR LOCAL LIBRARY, PARTICULARLY IF IT HAS A LOCAL INTEREST THEME.

Visit your local library and make a tentative enquiry to see if they'll pop a copy of your book to their shelves.

Again, as in book marketing idea #37, add a bookmark or a personal note explaining you're a local author and you'd love any word of mouth recommendations to friends and family.

Book Marketing Idea #66

START PROMOTING YOUR BOOK EVEN BEFORE YOU'VE FINISHED WRITING IT!

There are all kinds of ways to do this and it's super for generating a buzz about your book. You could set it up for pre-order too and create a VIP list for those who want to be the first to know when it's launched.

Use social media to:

1. share copies of your book cover
2. talk about the title/content/audience (text and video)
3. show a screenshot of your word count
4. or a behind-the-scenes pic of your first brainstorm.

Book Marketing Idea #67

CREATE & SHARE CONTENT THAT FOCUSES ON YOUR BOOK'S THEME.

Content marketing is my favourite way to promote my books and if you're an introvert like me, you'll probably prioritise it too.

If you've written a Journal Your Way to Happiness book (I have co-authored one by the way, *The Write Way to Be Happy Journal* - then create high quality articles for your website, Medium, LinkedIn, and guest blogs (ensure they're appropriate for whoever you're submitting to) which relate to journaling. Remember to add your book link in the bio (as mentioned in idea #17).

Book Marketing Idea #68

Make sure there's a call to action on all your pitching posts.

I spot this all the time. Missed opportunities. Don't share your book details or your Author Facebook page anywhere without a call to action.

- buy now if you want to learn x, y z
- join my Facebook group now if you want tips, ideas & advice about x, y z

Is heaps better than a 'Click Here' button, wouldn't you say? And it could end up in a sale, a sign-up to your email list or a new follower on your social media pages.

Book Marketing Idea #69

REGULARLY CHECK (AND SHARE) YOUR AMAZON AUTHOR CENTRAL PAGE TO SEE IF IT'S SHOWING ALL OF YOUR BOOKS.

One aspect of my writing/publishing business is to create lots of low content books and publish them on KDP. On a good month I will add 20 or so, and at the end of every month, I have a note in my diary to remind me to check that all the books I've published this month are showing on my Amazon Author Central page.

Sometimes they are already showing up. Other times I have to add them manually. It's worth the 15 minutes effort, though, and could result in a sale.

Book Marketing Idea #70

ADD YOUR BOOKS TO YOUR SOCIAL MEDIA HEADERS & BANNERS.

Show off your book covers in your social media headers and banners.

This makes them recognisable to people who follow you online and enables you to be consistent (remember that author branding idea I mentioned in #45?) across all your platforms.

When you've got another book in the pipeline and have decided on the launch date, add a 'Coming Soon' graphic too.

Book Marketing Idea #71

CREATE A BOOK POSTER OR FLYER AND PIN IT ON NOTICEBOARDS IN LOCAL COMMUNITY CENTRES, CHURCHES, AND YOUTH CLUBS.

Many local buildings are hired out now for all community groups to use: exercise classes, toddler gatherings, dancing, choir practice, weight loss groups etc.

And your ideal reader (or their friends/family) could be part of any of these groups.

Create an eye-catching poster or flyer (your book cover with a 'Local Author!' splash and a 'where to buy from' is enough) and pop it on the noticeboard. Who knows who'll see it?

Book Marketing Idea #72

CREATE A BOOKMARK TO HAND OUT AT NETWORKING SESSIONS INSTEAD OF A BUSINESS CARD.

Business cards are so last decade, right? So if you're a regular networker and you want to stand out from the crowd, invest in a small print run of bookmarks instead of business cards.

It's always a great ice-breaker and talking point, not just a useful marketing tactic.

Book Marketing Idea #73

ORGANISE A LOCAL SPEAKING EVENT WITH ANOTHER AUTHOR.

This can work well. I've seen it in action. An author from a nearby village had written his memoir and featured lots of local landmarks, events and places his readers would recognise. The other author (from five miles up the road) had written a semi-autobiographical novel based in the local area.

Their speaking event was intimate and successful and this relaxed type of book signing could be perfect for you too.

Do you know any authors in your locality who would team up with?

Book Marketing Idea #74

RESEARCH WHICH AUTHORS/PUBLISHING HOUSES TO FOLLOW ON YOUTUBE TO GET MORE PROMO IDEAS.

Why overcomplicate this marketing malarkey?
Follow a favourite indie author online and see if you could implement any of their tactics.

Unsure who to follow in your genre? Just check through the best-selling books on Amazon for that genre, click on the author names for the top ten books and start your research journey.

Be warned, you'll lose track of time doing this but it will be worth it.

Book Marketing Idea #75

JUMP ON PR OPPORTUNITIES BY LOOKING OUT FOR #JOURNOREQUESTS ON TWITTER.

All kinds of opportunities crop up if you follow the hashtag 'journorequest' (and other similar ones) on Twitter.

Today, for example, I've just seen a request for entrepreneurs to share advice for future start-ups for a journalist's article.

Now if you'd written a book about this subject and you were featured in the article ...

Book Marketing Idea #76

Make and share short & sweet videos of your book's interior.

Give your readers a chance to see inside your book by creating a video. Sometimes the Amazon 'Look Inside' feature isn't enough, particularly if you've created some kind of organiser or planner or workbook and readers want to see how much space there is to write inside, for example, before they buy.

Read through the contents page, talk about the good quality of the book, too. Every little insight helps.

Book Marketing Idea #77

BOOST YOUR BOOK MARKETING KNOW-HOW BY LISTENING TO PODCASTS.

You can't beat a good podcast to listen to while you're doing the chores, walking the dog or sweating down the gym.

My go-to favourites are:

- Joanna Penn – The Creative Penn
- Mark Dawson – Self-Publishing Formula
- Craig Martel & Michael Andarle: 50 books to 20k.

You can learn so much from people who have carved out successful publishing careers and it's a great way to fire up your motivation levels if your writing muse has vanished.

And that's a wrap!

Good luck!

Connect with Michelle

Love learning and chatting about self-publishing, writing and books? Follow me on social media for a regular fix.

- www.michelleemerson.co.uk
- www.facebook.com/selfpublishingservicesUK
- www.linkedin.com/in/selfpublishingservicesuk

Michelle

PS: If this book has given you heaps of new ideas and/or made a difference to how you see potential marketing opportunities, then please leave a review on Amazon or on my LinkedIn/Facebook profiles.

That would be much appreciated.

About Michelle

Michelle lives in beautiful Co Durham, England, with her son, daughter, hubby, and their bossy Shih Tzus, Buddy & Milo.

She's been passionate about writing since the age of 7 when Father Christmas gifted her a Victoria Plum Secret Diary, and has worked in publishing since the 1990s (before indie authors were even a thing!).

If she's not locked in her office/writing cave, you'll find her out walking, running or in a local café eating carrot cake and drinking latte.

Your Book Marketing Ideas & Results

It's helpful to monitor which of these promo ideas work for you because then you can build on the best bits. So grab a notebook or create an Excel spreadsheet to record your results.

If you'd like an extra special notebook, I have on one Amazon called *My Book Promotion Ideas* – you can grab a copy here: https://amzn.to/3wS9O67

It can save you a lot of time and effort in the future and help you create a successful book marketing strategy you can use for every book you publish.

Good luck!!

www.ingramcontent.com/pod-product-compliance
Lightning Source LLC
Chambersburg PA
CBHW070436220526
45466CB00004B/1700